GRAVE READING

RICHARD CARR

2014 Unsolicited Press Trade Paperback Edition
Copyright © 2014 Richard Carr
All Rights Reserved.
Published in the United States by Unsolicited Press.

ISBN: 069229029X
ISBN-13: 9780692290293

ACKNOWLEDGMENTS

Grateful acknowledgment
is made to the following publications in which
these poems first appeared:

"refused medicine," "a derangement,"
"dead dead" – *Chariton Review*
"cat" – *Pinyon*
"coat sleeves" – *Plainsongs*
"heroic endgame" – *Southwest Journal*

Contents

grave reading 1
vulgar in my throat 2
evening train 3
madonna 4
across the lawn 5
manifesto against old age 6
tongue to honey 7
heavenly muse 8
steer away 9
lighting the words 10
winter codex 11
refused medicine 12
burnt Eden 13
coat sleeves 14
squandered in the garden 15
still life 16
craft 17
maple seed 18
cat 19
her abundance 20
tornadic dance 21
fossil 22
pray and kill kneeling 23
machinery of nothing 24
highlife 25
a derangement 26
the prognosis 27
obit 28
her kiss 29
last address 30
the look 31
a boxer 32
hymns of delirium 33
dark at both ends 34

the scalpel 35
hanging laundry 36
next door 37
the night deep 38
a cricket song 39
tea 40
fang 41
ice-skating 42
dead dead 43
stars 44
tired world 45
on quiet days 46
heroic endgame 47
the farthest sky 48

GRAVE READING

grave reading

I sit on the low stone of my wife's grave
reading the newspaper out loud
courteous prince – notorious souse
cigars and crosses always brave

the hospital dedicated to blood and piss
we disbelieved – even the X-rays
now a mouse in the knotty pine cupboard
and the lips of plates and cups – kiss

diamond viewing window on the front door
my face a fog on the glass – looking back
passing hearse a magnet for iron-black eyes
my sandwich and chips a mess on the floor

vulgar in my throat

slitting a deer's belly – gut spilling
the psalms vulgar in my throat
all around the woods old widowers
push down their chins – close their coats

little green pricks come to prey on my tomato
in a kitchen pot – they dab the foliage brightly
a swatted fly stumbles on the table
takes flight on a wisp of air – but lightly

upstairs her nightgown flickers in the closet
its spider web necklace – the gift of a ghost
orange peels curl on a black lacquer tray
its vivid bamboo leaves – her brush strokes

evening train

the sorry cat watches a quivering leaf shadow
it does not understand wind and rain

I push the turnstile – defend my ring finger
a glossy magazine rides the evening train

playground sparrows shelter in the lilac hedge
shake their wings – cling with toothpick legs

the composer sighs in his bathtub – thunder
and distant rain – the cat tiptoes in and begs

madonna

opalescent madonna in the neighbor's garden
tending blue siberica in the wild springtime
a monster with a sagging belly I gape at her
the immaculate flowers deliquesce – I harden

for her I cut fruit bowls on my lathe
barefoot – the sharp shavings of poetry
fly against my robe – like Greek scrolls
I'd wash her feet – her bare body – bathe

in the wild springtime I linger in bed
eyes peeping like a newborn snake
vanilla coffee – a hooker in a warm car
then cold water howling in the showerhead

across the lawn

the woman next door contradicts me
opposes her garden to mine – her clean windows
curtained – to my fake shutters – one crooked
that one dangling shutter I love for its persistence

I will not move on – will not look across the lawn
but return to the worn-out carpet of my living room
to watch all-night poker on TV – my poker face sags
I will never move on from this place

convulsions of judgment and reversal wake me
when that woman comes knocking – needy
I'll drive her from the inferno to the pharmacy
and drop her half way to Heaven

manifesto against old age

dreams wasted – mirrors a waste of time
I fling aside the wet towel – and look
my body a manifesto against old age
its solemn declarations – tremble

tailored slacks unfit – fitted shirt unkempt
limbs no longer capable – of golf – handshakes
I play tetherball with the dead telephone
drop-kick the blaring radio across the yard

watching dog on the back step
teeters down onto the lawn
drawn to my outburst – old boy
we'll play fetch until we're tired

tongue to honey

the transatlantic cable crosses Lethe
furtively in both directions – thievish
prayers like tweezers – pluck a sliver
shirtsleeved in coach class – I shiver

mouthpiece crow scavenges thistledown
ringtones – annul my nervous sermon
buckled-in hijacker squirms in his seat
spider tormentor I – confess – deny defeat

to move on is – a forbidden beehive
box lunch a salad of fire and vertebrae
sick of motion – corpse gone runny
I'll taste – I'll touch my tongue to honey

heavenly muse

I drink in a crowded plaza ringed with cafés
postcard kiosks and a tour group praying
the ill-mannered artist and his bland patron
eat a silent lunch – neither thinks of paying

the photographer wants the shopkeeper to sweep
his leafy doorway – photo of a broom
I hide my drugstore camera under a napkin
snapshot of a garden – a church – my hotel room

pinging in the drain pipe – last night's rain
trickles through cobblestones like a lit fuse
the barmaid turns her back to mutter with a friend
aloof and irritable – ka-ching heavenly muse

steer away

engine loud as a Broadway musical
amped up high notes wowing every nerve
I aim to slam a concrete bridge abutment
but steer away – in yet another swerve

behind a veil of bamboo wallpaper
I'll learn to cook – to taste cheese – sip wine
take up guitar pottery watercolor – not bingo
though – all mere hobby – however refined

old men take up hobbies or put guns to their heads
or drive their well-earned sedans around town
until coffee time – I pull into my tidy garage
put my hand to my head – scratch – frown

lighting the words

twilight in the attic – boxes coats rafters dust
grainy in the halo-light and shadowy
interference – interplay of replica and original
a devil's candle alive but guttering in a gust

seashells and fossils in a shoebox – a time machine
hurtling through the brief epoch of my visit
I hold an old postcard close to my eye
sand grains clear – a beach microscopically clean

her letters – at the edge of the indigo void – recede
birthday kiss and anniversary tract – I composed
dangling guesses – folded notes passed in school
candle lighting the words – I kneel to read

winter codex

footprints recorded in the snow – a winter codex
illumination comes in spikes like icicles
in white sunlight – the crow all alchemy
perched on a wind-forgotten half-drifted bicycle

gazes meeting on the white lawn
boys look out windows – as they must
football is played in Buffalo no matter how cold
boots pushing like plowshares through the frozen crust

they rest – drum corps throbbing – for them
it is not possible to fall asleep on the snow
they flap their arms – generating surges of current
in white sunlight at my windowsill – hunched crow

refused medicine

droning moviegoer in the row behind
youth dragging his coat through the mall
the astronaut who saw ants on the peonies
same as anyone – felt ten miles tall

feedlot of Figaro cattle – warming up
backstage – the crow opposes health care
the president watches TV with his children
his helicopter shredding the night air

she refused medicine refused sugar
stabbed out her marble eye – the blight
to hear warbling in the abandoned barn
a dwindled spirit in shafts of light

burnt Eden

landscape painting of burnt Eden after the fall
trees black brush strokes

trotting coyote looking for a jackpot in the badlands
crow alights on a rock by the sea

lighthouse on the cliff saves a few lives
others succumb to the treacherous symphony

amplitude and gravity – death or a light nap
scorched wingtips of the gull – touch whitecaps

coat sleeves

her coat sleeves smell of tobacco – the old deep
remnant of her perfume – and a scalped fox
our old bar was a smoky hideaway run by two fatsoes
imperial and kind – clacking glasses of Scotch on the rocks

I've had enough to drink – my remaining friendships sit
    on shelves
like the athletic achievements of boyhood – the memories
    no longer fond
detainees crowded in the dark – I inspect the poisons under
    the kitchen sink
write a suicide note but assign no blame – only the willing
    are conned

her sickness was like a drunk – it could not be controlled
my sobriety is an unnatural metallurgy – transmuting all
    I know
in the copper forest – streams of steel band the hillsides
and I through bronze leaves – clang dully as I go

squandered in the garden

I wait in line at the hardware store
excited starlings gathering on the awning

bone meal squandered in the garden
I rake leaves in a light rain

I climb the ladder with effort
eaves troughs full of black muck

cat watching from the kitchen window
a worthless stone

still life

the conveyor belt carries my pecan pie
under its plastic dome
a tanned mummified face

the cashier has ripened – mellowed
become a still life
a bruised pear in a wooden bowl

she waits while I zip up my winter coat
touches her throat – as though I were the painter
pulling on his fingerless gloves

craft

part performance and part fraud
vandals play an encore in the alley
spray cans spelling out their demands
they want nothing – I do not applaud

abandoned amphitheater – bare stage
the canceled show a total loss – a dead art
in the marble house of government
the tyrant barricades against old age

I used to fear the A-bomb and the draft
now compose these limping tunes
once broke laws and wrote laws and sang it
now sing alone – retired to my craft

maple seed

I wander Sunday afternoons alone
carrying cut flowers for the grave
the seeker with a GPS – never fails
his quest is mapped out on his phone

I stop for coffee in a sleek café
a space station anchored in orbit
the bee – faster than any mind
checks his email – and spins away

the spinning maple seed faithfully departs
observing its sabbath in the sun
its tech the slow ticking of a hundred years
I deliver my flowers after dark

cat

cat – bones of driftwood – cluttered
in sleep – wrapped in glove leather
she – attacks a shoe with sharp nails
pulls out the laces – like purple entrails

cat – licking her back foot – immodest
in sleep – rolling over like a fur seal
she – wakes to sniff the woody air
licks and sleeps – in master's chair

cat – posed pharaonically – purring
in sleep – elongated desert carcass
she – rises like a seductive bloom
withdraws her gaze – owns the room

her abundance

coach hugged his clipboard
on the rainy sideline – we teenagers
indifferent – ruined his hopes
and mocked the queen on her float

years later she showed me a slug
sliding through wet leaves – the canopy
its afterlife – birdsong its angelic choir
but she saw light where I saw fire

the tumor was her last abundance
a holy grotto – carved in black stone
the gift shop all turquoise and crosses
calmed her fears – increased my losses

tornadic dance

the radio emits a warning – urgently
returns to music – the storm
veers like a shark to fresh blood
trapping me in the tool shed

I balance teacups on pencils
run circles with candles in both hands
put my eye to the whistling keyhole
the barbeque lifts off and crash-lands

I raise my voice against the wall of cloud
bolt for the house with a backward glance
dog-paddle in the river of wind
swirling my buoyant arms in tornadic dance

fossil

even a fossil enjoys political interpretation

chip away the useless crust

bone is construct – feather wisp a laceration

I sift down with the dust

pray and kill

battalions of dandelions march up the hill
I mow them down

weeds of a stained-glass summer pulled
I pray and kill kneeling

cantaloupe wedge shipwrecked in the sink
in a scree of toast crumbs roaches crawl

mouse a pretty damsel in a glue trap – help
no help – I thank no one for my bounty

machinery of nothing

the dog preens roughly – his brain
tells him everything he needs to know

he sprints along a mountain ridge
in a dream – I grope for the clock

bomb timer ticking – legs kicking like the dog
brain – machinery of nothing but pratfalls

I tumble through a bottomless closet
land on the roof of Hell feather-light

wind up the metronome of Paradise
too tight

highlife

the moon – drawn to riverbanks
crosses the night with wet feet
apple blossoms' precious confetti
celebrates itself – tipsy and sweet

cello song of the river barge fades
rumbling trucks shake the wheat
the city rocks to sirens and horns
and jackhammers dance in the street

the fatal miscalculations of youth
cruise downtown in suicidal heat
sanitary undersea prom in the gym
rehearses a highlife of cool deceit

a derangement

the sewing machine her anesthesia
and wine – the backwash of thought
the easy crucifixes of the crossword
her devotion – and a dove she bought

her labor a wheelbarrow full of doorknobs
the doctor a hair stylist – with closed eyes
her god an almighty stranger – her man
a scholar – worker of miracles and lies

the mutiny of her pregnancy – long due
a derangement of the body and the bride
a moaning tomcat and all the neighbors
at their windows – quietly the dove died

the prognosis

the prognosis flew past me like a meteor
sucked out all my breath
then veered round and stuck
a needle in my neck

a freight car full of rattling lightbulbs
somehow all survive
only to be screwed into sockets
and burned alive

my wine glasses merely sacramental
when I need to drink
I drink beer from the bottle
puke in the sink

obit

I wrote her obituary before she died
felt like a movie screen cowboy shooting his horse
there would be nothing left to tell

felt like I should take the dog out back
and shoot him too
to prove I could do it

the world – by which I mean
walking around the block
driving to the drug store

that world – felt like a bad habit
a small-town casino
where I had wasted the night

and all I could write was that I survived her
a horseless gambler standing on the dunes of morning
his losses and longings bleeding into the sands

her kiss

her smile a healed incision
she brushed her cheek against mine
instead of a kiss

last address

her suitcase slashed open
she walked in tall grass
I cried pinecones for her
for me – she wept sea glass

comfort of white buildings
made the sky seem clearer
I cried for her in private
darkly in my blue mirror

the umbrella her last address
her white blouse all undone
she fed on grass and leaves
for me – wept apples and sun

the look

God is a taciturn mechanic
a comb in his shirt pocket

I stamp my foot on the greasy
concrete floor

at the bus stop
a hard rain has ruined my shoes

he owes me a pair of shoes
I hiss

he applies correct torque
to the look in his rusted eye

and slams the hood
on any further communion

a boxer

a boxer with bloody teeth
punches me cockeyed
the better staggering brute
I vaunt the iron wreath

then the razor opens my eye
a needle stiffens my arm
I lose my footing in gore
drop to my knees – and die

hymns of delirium

busybody stoops at her window
helping no one – calls the cops
God's laws are beard bristles – his kiss
old womanish – a mistranslation of peace

hospitalized for my misdeeds
I chew my bandages – sleep swollen
betrayed – I brawl with the bedsheets
and sing the marching hymns of delirium

the hung jury swivel in their chairs
I survive the executions and earthquakes
but cannot be trusted – I await the night nurse
like a hostage restless for her touch

dark at both ends

the night watchman puts up his feet behind glass
his predecessor stepped on a nail
a marionette making shadows
acts out starting the car – pumping the gas

when the big car booming Jesus rumbles by
I cross myself for protection
and swallow the contradiction
a hard small pill that makes my throat go dry

I look in the mirror with diminishing affection
drink a glass of warm water
the hallway dark at both ends
the nightlight cannot contain the resurrection

the scalpel

the scalpel makes me transparent
keeps my organs cold

I wake for the visiting hour
the IV bag a sugary lens

drip of rain in a village hut
waters a frightening white orchid

released – I recover my bowling shirt
and the elevator chimes for the ride down

pain medication an exacting reminder
the cabbie won't help with my bag

hanging laundry

I mask my mouth against airborne pathogens
mosquitoes attack every other part of my flesh
hanging laundry I preach a gentle sermon
to the whipping sheets – urging them to be fresh

I press my ear against the bedroom wall
to hear the wind shoving against the roof
the Devil – his vast incorporeal unknown shape
flies toward some distant showdown and final proof

I ride the slow elevator up from the abyss
to wakefulness and a tentative light in the sky
I step outside – eyes open like hospital doors
dizzy in the calm – the sheets are white and dry

next door

next door a marriage is dissected over dinner
under an ornate light fixture blinking
asbestos and bad hair afflict the nation
sleepy protesters pepper-sprayed in the streets

playing in a twirling sprinkler soaking the lawn
boys and girls dance and collide
arteries pumping with laughter
long blockade lifted – my tin heart beats

I am happy – as a rodent
or seedpod lodged and waiting
sunshine breaking into the museum case
illuminates – a burnished relic with lost face

the night deep

a rain storm fills the cistern
fills me – makes the night deep
with the cold dark assurance
of the prophet's legendary sleep

the forlorn goat of dream
above the green terraces – dry lips pursed
climbs cautiously rock to rock
nibbles a shivering weed to scratch his thirst

to higher and higher strongholds
I climb – lightning lighting the dark way
past eggshells and small skulls
to find that tranquil lake – where the wise pray

a cricket song

the electric fence dips down to the creek
where the cattle find their way untended
through coarse alfalfa and scattered thistles
for a drink – all the wars have ended

the cattle pull their hooves from the mud
and walk slowly up the hill for the night
green flies resting on their piles of dung
at sunset – all wrongs made right

inside the dark barn the crickets creep
as the dust settles where the cattle bed
and when the big door is closed and bolted
they sing – a cricket song for all the dead

tea

railway journey – head bowed
mountain a solemn library
glacier is scripture – sudden
downcast joy of passing cloud

endless valley wind lifting up
the soaring bird – one alone
so wavers happiness – hot tea
lifted carefully in a white cup

temple bell – calls me to walk
across a bridge with lanterns
birch bark in springtime peels
happily – sky listens birds talk

fang

her hands flopped like two toads
through the knife drawer
I sniffed at her suicidal whims
wrestled her to the floor

saved her from the fang of a scissor
clenched in her fist
better a shard of champagne flute
to suit her delicate wrist

once I struck her hand against the sink
to knock the razor down the drain
she pushed the fractured bone against my chest
as though to make me feel her pain

ice-skating

ice-skating together for a date
surrounded by champions and damned
Prokofiev – we felt like children who don't know
how to love yet – or how to let go

I pulled her closer and we fell
pushed her away and we drifted apart
we locked hands and felt like children who
want to love – don't know what to do

champions lifted each other high above the ice
under loudspeakers playing the mournful
wolf march – and we felt like children who skate
in simple circles – in love and out late

dead dead

witness the doctor's banal finesse
when he pronounces the dead dead
his hand slides into his white pocket
saying what he cannot express

a redwing blackbird perches in his eye
his black Mercedes vandalized with red paint
a garbage truck ran over his dog
the dog did not die

Vermeer's blue reflections lit her face
then fell to goose gray
the doctor's carbon silence erased the rest
except some lilacs in a vase

stars

the stars she loved are muddled now
luminous jellyfish sunk in black tar
I wince to see them as they were
one star plucked from its constellation
rolls in my palm like a glassy cloud
I remember well the wish we made
the star – lights a memory of her face
struggles with itself – and flickers out

tired world

dead bird filled with rubies
yellow broom sweeps the walk

distant locomotive jolts to a start
smoke curl rising like a hawk

fireplace burns through the night
while the tired world sleeps

glowing logs spark and crumble
in the treetops – white stars creep

on quiet days

the stumps look like boot-tops
in the tall grass – the young
walk ahead of us barefoot
their voices bird-shrill and far-flung

their fate is ours to bear
their Monday voices in the valley
push against the schoolroom windows
escape the gym at the all-school rally

on quiet days the traffic moves along slowly
like dusty grazing bison
their dulcet fate is ours
to walk and bellow on the bald horizon

heroic endgame

I will pull up the covers of winter
one more season
play out the hard heroic endgame
against reason

then to Florida so hot and fraught
for a change
to dream of her freckled shoulders
and serene face

two chairs on the balcony await a storm
in drifting sand
I'll walk the endless empty beach
as we planned

the farthest sky

in a curdled mound of sea foam
a rainbowed bubble swells and pops
I look for her in the daily microcosms
of the tide pools and slippery rocks

on sand hills written out longhand
and in red miles of sunset dust
I look for her in the farthest sky
my eyes stung by the dry gusts

I look for her where I left her last
on a hilltop by the sea one day
buried in the cemetery of cremations
a neglected dune long blown away

Richard Carr's poetry collections are *Grave Reading* (Unsolicited Press 2014), *Lucifer* (Logan House Press 2013), *Dead Wendy* (FutureCycle Press 2012), *Imperfect Prayers* (Steel Toe Books 2012), *One Sleeve* (Evening Street Press 2011), *Ace* (Word Works Books 2009), *Street Portraits* (The Backwaters Press 2008), *Honey* (Gival Press 2008), and *Mister Martini* (University of North Texas Press 2008). His chapbooks include *Butterfly and Nothingness* (Mudlark 2004) and *Letters from North Prospect* (Frank Cat Press 1997). His honors include the Holland Prize for *Lucifer*, the FutureCycle Poetry Prize for *Dead Wendy*, the Washington Prize for *Ace*, the Gival Press Poetry Award for *Honey*, and the Vassar Miller Prize for *Mister Martini*. A former cemetery worker, hardware salesman, tavern manager, and systems analyst, he currently teaches English in Minneapolis.

www.ingramcontent.com/pod-product-compliance
Lightning Source LLC
Chambersburg PA
CBHW021027090426
42738CB00007B/929